Everyday
Ginger Recipes

Nancy Bellamy

DISCLAIMER

TABLE OF CONTENTS

PART 1:

Health Guide

INTRODUCTION TO GINGER

Ginger is a hot, fiery root with uneven beige skin and hard, succulent, pale yellow, white or red flesh, depending upon the type and variety. Ginger is most commonly used as a spice, either in a fresh or dried form and can also be ground to a powder or used in a crystallized form, especially for desserts. Fresh ginger is moist and juicy and has a pleasantly sharp but refreshing taste. It has an aromatic scent that makes it a perfect ingredient for sweet or savory dishes, whereas the dried powdered root has a much more sizzling and flavorsome contribution to the palette. Fresh ginger can also be conserved in sugar syrup or crystallized and coated in sugar – in these forms the spice is then known as stem ginger. Ginger or ginger root is the underground root of the plant 'Zingiber officinale', often used as a fragrant spice or for medicinal purposes and in some parts of the world, as a delicacy too. Ginger derives its botanical name from its Sanskrit name 'Singabera' which means 'horn shaped' which can often be a physical characteristic of ginger roots. Other close relatives of the ginger plant family are turmeric, cardamom, and galangal, also used as spices and for medicinal uses, predominantly in the Asian region.

This book contains health benefits and some recipes for both desserts and savory dishes as well as a recipe for ginger infused drinks for all to enjoy.

GINGER: A BRIEF HISTORY

Ginger is an age old inhabitant of the South- East Asian region, where it still features as a key ingredient in many cuisines. This delightfully fiery herb in all its various forms has been celebrated for thousands of years in many areas throughout the globe. The mention of ginger has been sighted in ancient Chinese, Indian and Middle Eastern works and writings, and has always been held in high praise for its fragrant, cookery and remedial properties. It was the Romans who imported ginger from China almost two thousand years ago to Europe, where its recognition in the European region remained predominantly central to the Mediterranean region until the Middle Ages, when its use and awareness spread throughout other countries. Ginger in some areas was and even to this day is a relatively expensive spice, and considered a delicacy; owing to the fact that it had to be imported from Asia, but still is in great demand. In an endeavor to make it more accessible, Spanish explorers introduced ginger production to the West Indies, Mexico and South America, and thus, approximately around the 16th century, these areas began to export the prized herb back to Europe.

Today, the greatest profitable producers of the ginger plant include Jamaica, India, Fiji, Indonesia and Australia.

Fresh young ginger can be delicately chopped, grated, and compressed to produce a ginger juice, or simply sliced/ diced to add aroma and flavor to food. In South-East Asia and the Indian subcontinent, pungent ginger, also known as 'adrak' is recurrently added to curry pastes and it is habitually cooked with fish dishes and stir-fry in China. In Europe, dried ginger is more commonly used in baking and desserts, which is a similar trend in northern England as well.

HEALTH BENEFITS OF GINGER

For many millennia, ginger has been used to cure numerous illnesses due to its powerful remedial and preventive effects. It has anti-emetic (treats vomit and nausea), pain-relieving, antioxidant, and anti-inflammatory characteristics. It also helps to reduce swelling, tenderness and pain due to its facility to slow down prostaglandin and leukotriene (inflammatory molecules) production and it has properties to reduce the effects of nausea and motion sickness. Its antioxidant properties, as well as the ability to stimulate cell death (apoptosis) and subduing certain protein results in ginger containing anticancer qualities. Composites found in ginger are known to curb allergic reactions. All these curative qualities make ginger a bank of health benefits.

Gastric Relief

Recent scientific studies have proven that ginger can eliminate effects of gastric distress as it has properties which assist in the removal of intestinal gas and soothes and settle down the intestinal tract, resulting in the elevation of any pain and discomfort. Studies also suggest that the use of ginger also assists with the prevention of any indicators of motion sickness, dizziness or cold sweats that may occur due to any unsettled gastric disturbances. The best method of yielding these results is to chew on ginger to keep down nausea due to aftermath of surgery or a side effect of chemotherapy amongst other conditions.

Allergy and Asthma Relief

Ginger is one of the most favored herbal home-made remedies to date, especially to cure ailments such as cough, sour throat and cold. Ginger has medicinal properties that can loosen and clear airways and help encourage the secretion of mucus. Consuming ginger also results in the suppression of and relief from various allergies, making it an effective natural antihistamine. A recommended remedy is a teaspoon of ginger juice combined with honey as a medicine for sour throat. This recipe mixed with a bit of fenugreek has proven to be a source of relief for asthma.

Ginger tea is also a tried and tested remedy for relief from congestion and sinus- related issues.

Morning Sickness Prevention

Studies conducted in the April 2005 issue of Obstetrics and Gynecology suggests that most women find ginger a much more effective form of medicine for relief from morning sickness than over the counter drugs. Ginger is required in a small quantity and doesn't have any side effects, which makes it a much safer option than most pharmaceutical drugs. Though a doctor should be consulted at all times, popular belief is that ginger has a strong anti- vomiting property that can be extremely helpful through the early and later stages of pregnancy. Another remedial quality of ginger is its ability to reduce menstrual pain for women who have known to consume it at the start of their period.

Relief from Aches and Pains

Ginger contains a very powerful anti-inflammatory composite called 'gingerols' that makes it a very effective pain killer, especially for aches and pains such as headaches and arthritis. Ginger contains an anti-inflammatory quality that can relieve joint ache and muscle tenderness. An effective way to achieve these results is to add ginger oil to baths and increase ginger intake with meals.

Ginger is a successful remedy for headaches as it reduces inflammation in blood vessels and relieves pain and discomfort.

Applying diluted ginger paste to the forehead is considered to be an effective method of reliving headaches.

Prevention against Growth of Cancer Cells

'Gingerol' is a compound found in ginger that gives it its distinguishing flavor as well as contains anti-inflammatory, antioxidant, and properties to possibly prevent the growth of cancer cells (anti-tumor), especially ovarian and colorectal cancer. Exposure to ginger can cause cell death, a process known as apoptosis and many research studies suggest that ginger can be a very effective weapon against cancer.

Overall, ginger is highly concentrated in substances and doesn't require a large quantity to be effective, which makes it a safe and accessible, remedial cure.

PURCHASING AND STORING GINGER

Ginger is easily found and is available in the produce section of all super markets as well as vegetable markets. Ginger is easily accessible in a dried powder form, mostly used in baking and desserts, as well as in a whole fresh form. Fresh ginger contains more 'gingerol' and anti-inflammatory properties than dried ginger and is also richer in flavor, especially useful when cooking savory dishes such as stir fry and curry pastes.

Fresh ginger is also available in two forms. A young ginger root, mostly found in Asian markets, which doesn't have a protective skin and requires no peeling. More mature ginger on the other hand, has a hard brown exterior that needs to be peeled. When purchasing ginger, always ensure that it is firm, juicy and doesn't have any traces of mold.

Ginger powder is widely available in supermarkets, but some further research into local vegetable markets or farm markets can often result in finding higher quality powder made with organic ginger. This might result in having a better flavor and an element of freshness to the dried spice.

Fresh ginger, if unpeeled, can be stored in the refrigerator for up to 3-4 weeks. If peeled, it can also be stored in a frozen form in the freezer; however, flavor wise that may not be the best option as fresh ginger can easily be purchased from any local market. Ginger powder can also be stored in a glass or plastic container in a cool, dry space, and depending on the temperature and humidity levels, can also be placed in the refrigerator as required. Ginger can also be preserved as a pickle, candied or in a crystallized form.

COOKING WITH GINGER

Ginger can be incorporated into food in its various forms. It can be chopped, pressed, used in its dried powder form, julienned or used as a paste combined with garlic mostly found in recipes of curry paste.

Below are some delicious sweet and savory recipes that incorporate ginger into food in wholesome scrumptious ways! These recipes can be used for breakfast, lunch or dinner.

PART 2:

Recipes

BREAKFAST RECIPES

Candied Ginger Crisps

Ingredients:

- 1 pound fresh ginger root
- 5 cups sugar
- 1 pound granulated sugar
- Non-stick spray

Method:

Firstly to prepare, spray a cooling rack with non-stick spray and place it in a pan lined with baking paper.

Peel the ginger root and cut it into 1/8 slices. Place the sliced ginger in a pan with 4 quarter water and boil over medium heat. Cover the pan with a lid and cook for approximately 35 minutes till the ginger seems tender and soft.

Once the ginger is tender, drain it and save ¼ of the cooked water along with it. Weigh the ginger and add an equal amount of sugar and ¼ of the cooked water back in a pan and boil on medium-high heat, stirring frequently. Bring the heat down to a medium but continue to stir until the water is almost evaporated (syrup begins to dry) and the sugar begins to crystallize. The process should take approximately 20 minutes.

The ginger then needs to be transferred to the cooking rack and the pieces spread apart. When the ginger is fully cooled, store in a jar or airtight container for up to 2 weeks.

Double Ginger Breakfast Crumble

Ingredients:

- 1 pound sliced Rhubarb
- 130gs brown sugar
- Zest and juice of one large orange
- 2 tbsp diced fresh ginger
- 2 tbsp diced crystallized ginger
- 45gs whole rolled oats
- 120gs plain flour (gluten- free is also an option)
- Pinch of sea salt
- 120gs diced cold butter

Method:

Firstly, preheat the oven at 180C/ gas mark 4. In a medium sized pan, place the rhubarb and half the brown sugar to add into it. Add 1 tbsp crystallized ginger and 1tbsp of fresh ginger into the pan and then incorporate the orange juice and zest. Bring to boil on a medium low heat with the lid on the pan.

Soften the rhubarb by simmering the mixture on a low heat for a few minutes, and then ladle the compote onto an oven proof dish.

Take a bowl and add flour, butter, rolled oats, the remaining gingers, brown sugar, and salt and blend them in together with your hands to make a fine crumble for the topping.

Spread the crumble evenly over the rhubarb compote and bake in the oven for 40 minutes until the crumble is golden brown. Take the dish out from the oven and when it has cooled slightly, serve with a dollop of yogurt, vanilla ice cream, whipped cream or custard.

Hay Maker's Ginger Switchel

Ingredients:

- ¼ cup cider vinegar
- ¼ cup molasses
- ¼ cup minced fresh ginger
- ¼ honey/ maple syrup
- ¾ cup lemon juice
- 9 cups water, divided
- Fresh berries and lemon slices

Method:

Mix the fresh ginger with 3 cups of water and bring to boil in a pan on medium-high heat for 2 minutes. Then set the pan aside, cover it with a lid and let the mixture cool for 15 minutes.

Strain the water with the help of a strainer, ensuring the any solid ginger particles are removed, then mix in the honey and molasses into the ginger water until properly infused. Mix in the rest of the water, lemon juice and vinegar into the ginger water and chill for a couple of hours or overnight.

Serve with lots of ice and use lemon slices, mint leaves or berries for garnish and extra flavor. This is a great breakfast drink to have on a hot summer day.

Pancakes with Ginger-Maple Syrup (Mango)

Ingredients:

- 1 egg
- 1 ½ cups whole milk
- 1 cup pure maple syrup
- 2 tbsp extra virgin coconut oil
- 2 tbsp baking powder
- 1 ripe mango (peeled)
- 1 tbsp raw honey
- 1 ½ cups white wheat flour
- 1 tsp baking soda
- ½ tsp salt
- ½ tbsp ground cardamom
- 2 tsp grated ginger

Method

The first step is to start on the pancake syrup. To make the syrup, warm the maple syrup on a small pan on the stove till it is properly warm to touch and then add the grated ginger into it and stir to properly integrate throughout. Take the syrup off the heat and set aside to let the flavors infuse with each other.

To make the pancake mix, peel the mango and add all the pulp to a blender along with the honey, egg, coconut oil and milk and blend on high speed for several seconds. Pour the mango mixture into a larger mixing bowl. Now add the flour, salt, cardamom, baking powder and baking soda in another mixing bowl and then add the dry mix into the mango mixture and smooth together until it becomes one velvety mixture.

Heat a medium sized pan or griddle and using a ¼ measuring cup, scoop batter almost to the full cup and pour onto the pan or griddle. Flip the pancake when little bubbles appear on one side and cook till they are golden brown. Strain the ginger bits out of the maple syrup with a strainer. Serve slightly warmed with pancakes.

Ginger Orange Smoothie

Ingredients:

- 2 small oranges (peeled and cut)
- ½ cup low-fat milk
- 2 tsp sliced ginger
- ½ medium banana
- 1 tbsp unsweetened almond butter
- 4 ice cubes

Method

Add all the ingredients in a high- speed blender and blend for a few minutes till all the ingredients are smoothly incorporated. Serve cold and garnish with orange shavings.

<u>Lemon Ginger Granola</u>

<u>Ingredients:</u>

- ½ cup honey
- ½ brown sugar
- Juice from 3 lemons
- 3 cup oats
- ¼ cup flax seeds
- 1 cup almonds (slivered)
- Zest from 3 lemons
- ½ candied ginger (chopped into small pieces)
- 1 tsp grounded ginger
- ¾ tsp fresh grated ginger
- 2-4 chopped dates (optional)
- Oil/ non-stick spray

Method

To start off, preheat oven at gas mark 4-5 and line two baking trays with foil and cover them with oil or non-stick spray and set aside.

In a small pan, mix together the brown sugar, honey, lemon juice and lemon zest and the ground and grated ginger. Bring to boil and let it simmer till the sugar is fully incorporated and then take off the heat and let it cool for a while. Take a large glass bowl and add the oats, flax seeds, almonds and dates (optional) into the bowl, then add the wet mixture and mix till the dry ingredients are fully coated.

Evenly spread the on the two baking trays and bake for almost an hour in the oven. Make sure to check the granola every 15 minutes and stir to insure an even cook. Once the liquid had evaporated and the granola looks cooked, take out the trays and cool the granola, and then add in the candied ginger and mix (you might have to break the larger granola chunks). Store the granola in a glass jar or metal tin.

<u>Ginger Muffins</u>

<u>Ingredients:</u>

- 3 ounces unpeeled ginger root
- 8 tbsp unsalted butter
- 2 cups all-purpose flour
- ¾ cups sugar
- 2 eggs
- 1 cup buttermilk
- 3 tbsp additional sugar
- 2 tbsp lemon zest (grated)
- ¾ tsp baking soda
- ½ tsp salt

Method

Before starting, preheat oven at 375° F.

Cut ginger root into tiny pieces using a food processor or hand-mince it. It should measure approximately 1/3 cup or more. Take a skillet, put in ginger and ½ cup sugar, and cook until the sugar melts. Keep the heat medium and stir continuously. When done, take it off and let it cool.

Take a bowl and put in 3 tbsp of sugar and lemon zest into it. Using your hands, rub the zest and sugar until the zest releases oil. Add this to ginger concoction.

Take a mixing bowl, and put butter and the remaining sugar in it. Mix them until smooth and then add eggs to eat while continuing to beat it. Next, add buttermilk and create a fine blend. Now add salt, baking soda and flour and make a smooth mix. At last, add the ginger concoction to it and beat it to make a smooth batter.

With a spoon, put the batter into a greased muffin tray and put it into the oven. Bake until a tester is perfect which would usually take 15 to 20 minutes and serve hot.

Ginger, Banana and Strawberry Smoothie

Ingredients:

- 6 strawberries
- ½ tsp chopped ginger root
- 1 pitted peach
- ½ banana cut into chunks
- 2/3 cup evaporated milk
- 1 tsp vanilla extract
- Ice cubes as required

Method

Place all ingredients in a blender and blend together while putting ice cubes one at a time. Pour out the smoothie into glass and garnish with ground cinnamon. Serve cold.

Ginger Honey Tea

Ingredients:

- 1 green tea bag
- 1 tbsp honey
- 2 tbsp orange juice
- 2 tbsp grated ginger
- 6 oz. hot water

Method

Put the tea bag in the water and steep for 2 minutes. Putting the ginger in a cheesecloth, squeeze its liquid into the tea. Add orange juice and honey. Mix it well and serve warm or cold (with ice).

Ginger-Spiked Lassi

<u>Ingredients:</u>

- 1 tbsp peeled and grated ginger
- 1 tsp toasted and crushed cumin seeds
- 200 ml natural yogurt
- 200 ml cold water
- A pinch of salt
- Ice cubes as required

<u>Method</u>

Pour the cold water and yogurt in the blender, then toss in ginger, salt, and cumin seeds. Then blend the mixture and add ice cubes if required.

LUNCH RECIPES

Ginger Loaf

Ingredients

- 2 tbsp ground ginger
- 1 ½ cups flour
- 1 ½ tsp grounded cinnamon
- ½ tsp baking soda
- ¼ tsp grounded cardamom
- ¼ tsp grounded cloves
- ½ cup molasses
- ½ cup butter milk
- 2 eggs
- 1/3 cup dark brown sugar

- ½ tsp salt
- ½ cup unsalted butter

Method

To make ginger loaf, firstly preheat the oven to 170 °C, gas mark 3-4 and grease a load tin, preferably a 9 inch one. Combine all the dry ingredients together in a bowl.

Cream together the butter and sugar using an electric whisk till nice and fluffy, then add in the molasses and the eggs. Mix these together thoroughly and then add in the butter milk. If the mixture appears a bit curdled, this is alright at this stage. Add the dry ingredients to the mixture and beat together till everything is properly combined and there is a smooth batter.

Pour the mixture into the tin and let it bake for 45-55 minutes and then let the gingerbread cool in the tin for 15 minutes before taking it out of the tin and placing it on a cooling rack.

Quick Yogurt and Ginger Snack

Ingredients:

- About 5-6 ginger biscuits
- 1 tbsp lemon juice
- 1 green apple
- 150 ml natural yogurt
- ½ tbsp caster sugar

Method:

To make this quick and healthy snack, place the ginger biscuits in a plastic bag and crush them with a rolling pin. Then put a portion of the crushed biscuits into the bottom of a dessert bowl. Grate the apples into another bowl and squeeze in some lemon juice and add some caster sugar for taste. Add the apples on top of the biscuits. Scoop a dollop of natural yogurt on top of the apples and sprinkle with the remaining biscuit crumbs. Chill for 2 hours or serve immediately, as preferred.

Chocolate Ginger Brownies

Ingredients

- 3 oz dark chocolate (broken into pieces)
- 2/3 cup plain flower
- 1 cup caster sugar
- ¼ cup cocoa powder
- 1 tsp fresh grated ginger
- ½ cup unsalted butter (extra for greasing)
- ½ tsp nutmeg
- ¼ tsp salt
- ½ nutmeg
- ½ ginger powder
- 1/8 tsp ground cloves

Method

Preheat the oven to 170°C, gas mark 3 - 4 and grease a baking tray, an option would be to use a 20 cm square baking tin. Melt the chocolate and butter in a pan on low heat and then set aside from the heat and allow cooling.

Stir in all the other ingredients and mix until smooth, then pour the mixture into the pan and bake for 30 minutes. Once baked, allow the brownies to cool in the pan and serve however you like.

Sweet Potato and Ginger Soup

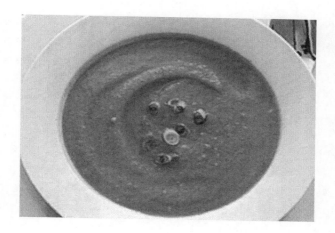

Ingredients:

- 4-5 medium sweet potatoes
- 1 tbsp vegetable oil
- 4 tsp finely chopped fresh ginger
- 4 thinly sliced green onions
- 3 ½ cups chicken broth
- Salt and ground pepper to taste
- ½ cup plain yogurt
- 2 tbsp fresh cilantro chopped
- 2 tbsp lemon juice
- Lemon wedges for garnish

Method:

Heat the oven to 200°C, gas mark 6. Wash the sweet potatoes, prick them all over with a fork and cook in the oven for 45 minutes or till they are soft. In a small soup pan, on medium heat, warm the vegetable oil and add the green onions to it. Sauté the onions till they are soft which should take about 3 minutes, then add 3 teaspoons of ginger and stir for another extra minute or so until it has a nice aroma, then pour in the chicken broth and bring to boil. Now reduce the heat and for 15 minutes let the mixture simmer.

Once the sweet potatoes are tender in the oven, remove them from the oven and allow them to slightly cool. Cut the sweet potatoes in half length wise and scoop out the middle part and add it to the broth. After the broth mixture has cooled, transfer it to a blender and mix until rich and velvety. To add more flavor squeeze in the lemon juice and remaining teaspoon of ginger and some salt and pepper to taste. Use the lemon wedges and cilantro for garnish and a dollop of yogurt when serving is a good option.

Ginger Almond Biscotti

Ingredients:

- 2 eggs
- 9.5 oz. plain flour
- 4 oz. softened butter
- 2 tbsp treacle
- 4.5 oz. brown sugar
- 1 ½ tsp baking powder
- ¼ tsp salt
- 4 oz. chopped crystallized ginger
- 3 oz. toasted and flaked almonds
- 2 tbsp ground ginger
- 2 tsp freshly grated ginger

Method:

Heat the oven to 180°C, or gas mark 4.

Put butter and brown sugar in a mixing bowl and beat until the mixture is fluffy and light. One by one, add the eggs while beating the mixture continuously. Lastly, add treacle and beat well until it forms a smooth fine mixture.

In another mixing bowl, mix flour, ground ginger powder, salt and baking soda. Add this to the butter and egg mixture and mix it well. Add almonds, crystallized ginger and fresh ginger to the mixture and blend it until it gets smooth.

Divide the mixture into two equal parts and form two dough logs, each about 5 cm wide and 20 cm long. Place these logs on an already lined baking tray and let it bake for about 30 minutes. After that, let it cool for 5 minutes.

Cut the logs into biscotti slices carefully and put them on the baking tray again, turning them over on sides. Leave them to bake for another 10 minutes. Take out and let them cool. Serve as snacks.

Fish Cakes with Ginger and Herbs

Ingredients:

- 4 skinless and boneless fillets of firm white fish
- 2 eggs
- 3 g breadcrumbs
- 2 tsp sunflower oil
- 25 g peeled and grated ginger
- Grated zest of 1 lemon
- 25 g chopped dill
- 15 g chopped mint leaves
- 3 finely crushed garlic cloves
- 10 g chopped tarragon
- 1 tsp ground cumin

- ½ tsp ground turmeric
- 8 long green peppers
- Salt and black pepper as required

Method:

Preheat the oven to gas mark 6 or 200° C. Slice and chop the fish into very small and fine pieces, just about 1-2 mm in size. Put them in a bowl and add ginger, garlic, herbs, lemon zest, eggs, breadcrumbs, ground spices, salt and black pepper. Mix all the ingredients well and make 12 separate patties from them.

Take an ovenproof pan and place it on high heat. When the pan gets hot, grill green peppers on it for 15 minutes, until the skin gets charred. Take them off and let them cool. Wipe the pan.

Add sunflower oil to the pan next, and sear the fish cakes. Let them cook for 4 minutes, turning once in between. Now place the pan into the preheated oven and bake for 8 more minutes. Take them out and serve hot with grilled peppers.

Broccoli with Ginger

Ingredients:

- 6 cups (1 pound) trimmed and chopped broccoli crowns
- 4 tsp minced ginger
- 2 tbsp minced garlic
- 1 tbsp rice vinegar
- 1 tbsp canola oil
- 1 tbsp fish sauce
- 3 tbsp water

Method:

Take a large skillet and put canola oil in it. Keep the heat medium-high. When the oil has heated, add ginger and garlic to it and cook for about 30 seconds. When it gets fragrant, add broccoli crowns to it and cook for 2 minutes, until the broccoli turns bright green, and keep stirring.

Drizzle it with water and fish sauce and bring down the heat to medium. Cover the skillet properly and let it cook until the broccoli is tender. At last, add the rice vinegar and turn off the flame immediately. Serve hot.

Ginger Orange Bulgur

Ingredients:

- 1 cup rinsed bulgur
- 2 oranges
- 2 cloves minced garlic
- 2 tbsp fresh ginger, minced
- 2 tsp canola oil
- 2 tsp brown sugar
- 1 tbsp soy sauce
- ¼ tsp salt
- 2/3 cup scallions, chopped
- 1/3 cup almonds, slivered

Method:

Take 1 orange and zest it; keep the zest aside. Now juice both the oranges. The juice should measure up to 1 ½ cup total. Add water if needed to complete the measure.

Place a heavy saucepan on medium-high heat and heat oil in it. Add ginger and garlic and cook for about 30 seconds, stirring, until fragrant. Now add bulgur and coat it properly. Add orange juice, salt and brown sugar to the saucepan and stir it for a few seconds.

Bring it to a simmer. Bring down the heat slightly to maintain the simmer. Cover the pan and let it cook for about 20 to 25 minutes, until the bulgur turns tender and the liquid is absorbed.

Add scallions, orange zest and soy sauce to the saucepan after the bulgur is tender and mix gently. Use a fork to fluff it up. In a separate skillet, toast the almonds on low heat until they turn light golden, for about 2-3 minutes. Serve the bulgur sprinkled with the roasted almonds.

Peanut-Ginger Sauce with Tofu

Ingredients:

For Sauce:

- 2 cloves minced garlic
- 2 tsp minced ginger
- 2 tsp soy sauce
- 2 tsp honey
- 1 tbsp vinegar (white or rice)
- 5 tbsp water
- 4 tbsp smooth peanut butter

For Tofu and Vegetables:

- 14 ounces tofu, extra-firm and water-packed
- 4 sliced scallions
- 2 tsp extra-virgin olive oil
- 1 ½ cups sliced mushrooms
- 4 cups baby spinach

Method:

In a small bowl, mix peanut butter with water, vinegar, honey, ginger, soy sauce and garlic, and whisk well together. Keep the sauce aside.

Drain, rinse and pat dry the tofu. Cut the slice into 8 slabs, each about ½ inch thick, and then cut into small cubes. In a large non-stick skillet, heat the oil and add tofu. Spread it in a single layer and cook it until it turns golden brown from one side without turning it over. Then, turn it over and cook until all sides are golden brown.

When the tofu is cooked well from all sides, add scallions, mushrooms, spinach and peanut butter sauce to the skillet. Cook until the vegetables are ready and keep stirring for about 2 minutes, and then take it off. Serve hot.

Ginger Fried Rice

Ingredients:

- 4 large beaten eggs
- 3 tsp peanut oil, divided
- 1 bunch chopped scallions
- 1 tbsp fresh ginger, minced
- 1 cup frozen peas
- 1 cup bean sprouts
- 3 tbsp oyster sauce
- 3 cups long-grain brown rice, cold cooked

Method:

Place a large non-stick skillet over medium-high heat and put oil in it. Add well-beaten eggs and cook well; keep stirring and scramble the eggs well. Take them out in a plate and set aside.

Add the remaining oil to the skillet and put scallions and ginger in it. Fry until the ginger is fragrant for about 1-2 minutes. Then, add peas and rice to it. Cook until they start sticking to the pan, then add oyster sauce, sprouts, and fried eggs to it. Toss everything together for about 2 minutes and serve immediately.

DINNER RECIPES

Exotic Chicken Ginger Stew

Ingredients

- 1 pound chicken (cut into cubes)
- Small piece of ginger (julienned)
- 1 tbsp sesame oil
- 4 cloves garlic (thinly sliced)
- ½ cup dry sherry
- 1 1/4 ounce canned chicken broth
- 2 tbsp soy sauce
- 1 ½ cups water
- 1 bunch of mustard greens
- 1 tbsp chili sauce

Method:

To prepare this dish, heat a pan with peanut oil over medium heat and cook the chicken. Stir the chicken for about 6-7 minutes to ensure it is cooked properly, and then put it aside in a plate.

In a pot, add the ginger and the garlic and cook for a few seconds, then add the sherry and cook till the sherry is almost evaporated and the garlic and ginger turn brown. Now add the chicken broth and water to the pot and bring to boil over high heat and boil for about 5 minutes. Now add the chili sauce, soy sauce and chard greens and cook till the greens are tender. Now add the cooked chicken into the broth mixture and cook for another 2-3 minutes. Serve in a bowl; add steamed white rice for more texture if required.

Ginger Coconut Chicken

Ingredients:

- 4 boneless/skinless chicken breasts
- 2 tbsp fresh minced ginger
- 4 minced medium garlic cloves
- ½ tsp salt
- 1 tbsp yellow split peas
- 1 tsp coriander seeds
- ¼ cup coconut milk
- 1-2 dried red chilies
- 2 tbsp fresh chopped cilantro

Method:

For 2-3 minutes, toast the chilies, split peas and coriander seeds in a small skillet, shaking the pan till the peas turn a reddish brown, and the chilies look a little burnt. Cool the mixture in a plate and then place in a grinder to grind till the mixture becomes a peppery powder.

Take a low glass dish and add coconut milk, grinded powder, salt, garlic, ginger, and cilantro and soak the chicken in the mixture, coating it properly and either covering and refrigerating it for 30 minutes or leaving it to marinate overnight.

When ready to cook, take a broiler and spray a broiler rack with non-stick spray. Place the chicken (with marinade) on the rack and cook both sides for 5-6 minutes each and until the chicken is no longer pink.

<u>Ginger Prawns with Vegetables</u>

<u>Ingredients:</u>

- ½ pound broccoli
- ½ snow peas
- ½ an onion chopped
- 3-4 scallions
- 1 piece of fresh garlic (peeled)
- 3 gloves of garlic (peeled)
- 1 tbsp sesame oil
- 1 tbsp black bean chili sauce
- 1 pound chow mien noodles
- ¼ cup peanut oil
- ¼ cup peanut sauce
- 1 pound cleaned prawns

Method:

To start off, cut the scallions into thin slices and mince the ginger and garlic. To prepare the vegetables cut the broccoli into equal pieces and prepare the snap peas into julienne strips. Boil them in water for a few minutes, and then add the ice cold water to stop the cooking process and set aside.

For the noodles, boil 2 cups of water and add in the noodles for 4-5 minutes and bring to boil. Drain the water and toss the noodles with the sesame oil and the black bean chili sauce and put in a serving bowl.

For the prawns, heat the peanut oil on medium heat in a deep sauté pan. When the oil is hot, add in the chopped onions and sauté for 2 minutes. Then add the prawns to the oil and sauté for another minute, followed by the minced ginger and garlic and sauté for another 1-2 minutes. Now add the broccoli and scallions and stir the pan for another minute and then add in the peanut sauce and cook till well heated and mixed properly. Add the prawn mixture to the noodles and garnish with blanched snow peas. Serve hot.

Ginger and Pineapple Stir- Fry

Ingredients:

- 400g beef steaks (thinly sliced)
- 4 spring onions (julienned)
- 200gs pineapple cut into chunks
- 2 tbsp soy sauce
- 1 tbsp chili sauce
- 2 tbsp brown sugar
- 1 tbsp white wine vinegar
- 1 piece ginger thinly sliced
- Handful of coriander leaves
- Greens and rice for serving
- 2 tsp vegetable oil

Method:

Put the steak slices in a bowl and add sugar, soy sauce, chili sauce and vinegar to the steak, mix well and let them infuse for 10 minutes.

Heat a wok on medium heat and add a teaspoon of oil, and lift the steak from the mixture and sear it in the oil and then set it aside again. Add another teaspoon of oil and sauté the ginger in it. Then add the pineapple and onions into the oil as well. Now add the steak back to the wok and stir for about a minute, and then add the remaining marinade back into the wok. Keep cooking the ingredients till there is a thick sauce and everything is cooked thoroughly. Garnish with coriander and serve with boiled/ steamed rice or greens.

<u>Stir-Fry Ginger Chicken</u>

<u>Ingredients:</u>

- 1 ½ pounds boneless chicken breasts, cut into large cubes
- ½ cup sliced scallions
- 1 large thinly sliced onion
- ½ cup fresh ginger, cut into julienne sticks
- 2 cloves minced garlic
- 2 tbsp canola oil
- 2 tbsp sugar
- 2 tbsp white vinegar
- ¼ cup soy sauce

Method:

Soak the thinly-cut ginger in cold water. Leave it for 10 minutes and then drain well. Take a skillet and heat canola oil in it on high heat. Fry the chicken pieces for about 6 to 8 minutes until they are brown from all sides. Take them out and set aside.

Using the same skillet, fry onion, ginger and garlic for about 8 to 10 minutes, until the onion turn slightly brown. Now, add sugar, vinegar and soy sauce to the skillet. Turn the heat to high and cook for 3 to 4 minutes, until it thickens. Now add the fried chicken pieces and cook for a few minutes to heat the chicken. Stir in scallions and remove from heat immediately. Serve hot.

Ginger with Roasted Beets

Ingredients:

- 2 ½ fresh beets, medium-sized
- 1 ½ tbsp minced ginger
- 2 tbsp extra-virgin olive oil
- 2 ½ tbsp balsamic vinegar

Method:

Heat the oven at 450° F. Take a cookie sheet and line it with foil properly. In a small mixing bowl, put vinegar, olive oil and ginger and mix well.

Trim the stems of the beets to 1 inch and then cut the beets in half. Arrange the beets on the cookie sheet with foil, keeping the cut side up. Except the stems, brush all parts of beets with the ginger mixture and put it into the oven. Keep the beets uncovered and bake for 20 to 25 minutes, until the beets go very tender. Take them out and serve warm.

Roasted Chicken with Ginger and Lime

Ingredients:

- 8-10 chicken pieces
- 2 freshly squeezed limes
- 3 garlic cloves, crushed
- 2 tbsp ginger, freshly grated
- ¼ cup soy sauce

Method:

In a mixing bowl, put together ginger, garlic, lime juice and soy sauce to create a marinate mix. Take a baking dish, and put the chicken pieces in a single layer. Pour over the marinate mix and turn the chicken pieces until all the ingredients mix well. Cover the baking dish with a plastic wrap and put it in the freezer. Let it rest for at least 2 hours. You can also leave the chicken to marinate overnight.

Preheat the oven at 375° F. Put the marinated chicken into the oven and cook well for about an hour, until the chicken in not pink from anywhere. Take it out and serve immediately with any side dish.

Beet Soup with Coconut Milk and Ginger

Ingredients:

- 3 large red beets
- 1 can low fat coconut milk
- 3 cloves chopped garlic
- 1 tbsp chopped ginger
- 1 large onion, diced
- 1 tbsp olive oil
- 5 cups vegetable stock, divided
- ¼ tsp ground black pepper
- ½ tsp salt
- Parsley for garnish

Method:

Peel and cut the beets into ¼ inch cubes. Take a large cooking pot and put oil into it, keeping medium-high heat. Put the onion and sauté it for around 5 minutes. Now add ginger and garlic and cook for another 5 minutes while stirring often. Next, add beets and 4 cups of vegetable stock. On high heat, bring it to boil once, and then lower the heat to let it simmer. Cook for about 20 minutes until the beets are tender.

Using a blender, puree the soup and add the remaining cup of stock if required for your desired consistency. While keeping the heat low, add salt, pepper and milk to the soup. Turn the heat off and pour the soup in bowls. Garnish with parsley and serve hot.

<u>Vegan Gingerbread Cake (Spicy)</u>

<u>Ingredients:</u>

- 2 ½ cup all-purpose flour
- ¼ cup blackstrap molasses
- 1 cup dark corn syrup
- 3 oz finely grated ginger
- ¾ cup sugar
- 1 tsp ground cinnamon
- 1 cup peanut oil
- 1 cup water
- ¼ tsp ground cloves
- ¼ tsp salt
- ¼ tsp ground black pepper
- 3 tsp egg replacement
- 2 tsp baking soda

Method:

Heat the oven at 350 F. Chop the fresh ginger very finely.

In a mixing bowl, put the molasses, sugar, peanut oil and corn syrup and mix well. Keep it aside. In another bowl, whisk flour, salt, pepper, cinnamon and clove together. Keep it aside too.

Boil the water in a pan and then add baking soda to it. Add this boiling water to the molasses mixture and mix well. Add the grated ginger to this mix and whisk everything together finely. Now add the dry ingredients to this hot mix and mix together until it forms a smooth batter. Lastly, add the egg replacement mixed with 3 tbsp of water to this batter and mix until everything comes together smoothly.

Pour this batter into muffin molds or cake pans, and let them bake for about 20 minutes, until the cake turns soft, fluffy and gentle to touch. Take it out, let it cool and then serve.

<u>Ginger-Flavor Mojito</u>

<u>Ingredients:</u>

- 2 ½ oz spiced rum
- 3 tsp white sugar
- 25 fresh mint leaves
- 1 chopped lime
- Ginger beer for the top up
- Sliced fresh ginger for garnish

Method:

Put mint leaves, lime and sugar onto a cutting board. Using one end of a rolling pin, slightly mash and muddle them together. When the ingredients are mashed properly, add spiced rum and crushed ice and place it all in the glass. Mix well with a tall spoon. Top it up with ginger beer and fill the glass to the brim. Garnish with sliced ginger.

CONCLUSION

To conclude, ginger is not only an aromatic and fiery vegetable that elevates the taste of both sweet and savory food, but also has numerous health benefits that have been outlined in great detail above, as well as many recipes that incorporate ginger as a key ingredient and can be easily compiled at home at any time.

Ginger has several health benefits as well as several preventive properties, which is why it should ideally be used as an essential part of an individual's daily diet. It is often not required in large quantities to reap its remedial rewards. The 'gingerol' compound found in ginger is most beneficial as an anti-inflammatory, anti-tumor and anti-gastric cure and can prove to be an excellent home remedy for aches and pains.

Above there are several breakfast, lunch and dinner recipes that use significant amounts of ginger for flavoring and of course provide health benefits as well. These recipes can be used in an interchangeable order as and when desired and the dessert recipes can be enjoyed on many festive occasions and heartily enjoyed!

Printed in Great Britain
by Amazon.co.uk, Ltd.,
Marston Gate.